AF416252

FORGET

Second edition. January 2021. Copyright © 2020 Jose Cortes. Written by Jose Cortes. Cover art by Lauren Leung.

FORGET

A CHAPBOOK BY

JOSE CORTES

COVER ART BY

LAUREN LEUNG

To you, who may have already forgotten.

WHEN YOU SIT AT THE PIANO

I know that when the house stops creaking
and the birds outside sit on the windowsill,
that you must be at the piano.

It starts off with a single note floating,
for a moment's breath, alone.
Then its brothers arrive, sisters join,
lovers old and new emerge
to take part in this moment's
glimpse of ecstasy.

I can feel everything you play
as I watch you from the audience
that is our couch. Your lips curl in,
your forehead creases, and your hands
glaze over the keys like clouds
moving quickly on a winter day.

You are in unmistakable pleasure
as you make every feeling in the world,
every drop of lust and terrifying tears
come to life at your fingertips.

And so am I. There is no greater gift
you can give me than to make me
quiet my own breath.

The birds and I have agreed on that.
Even when you say that you need practice,
we will be silent, fearful that you may start
playing at any moment, and we will
find ourselves stolen of a drop of bliss.

I REMEMBER

I told myself that when I died, I'd think about
my childhood. I told myself that I would see
my dark blue room, that I would hear the bells
of mass, and that I'd feel the pain of growing up.

I had convinced myself of it. I was only waiting
for the perfect way to say goodbye.

So tell me then, why you won't leave my mind?
I can see you smiling up at me, I can hear you laugh
and moan, I can even feel your body resting on my own.

You're all that I can think about as I fall onto the grass,
the shots still ringing in my ears. You're the last thing
I remember as a siren starts to cry in the far-off distance.

A DANCE

On the day this all began,
we should have danced.
We should have gone into the ballroom,
introduced our souls and greeted our hearts.
We should have known our youth,
known the curse it carried inside,
like a romantic cover slipped over
a grisly horror novel.
And on the day everything ended,
we should have danced.
For here was our lesson,
a lesson of dancing alone
to a rhythm meant for two.
We've had our past, let's have our present.
Let's have a dance, a one two three waltz
or just move our bodies and swing our arms.
Let's have our dance.
Let's have our gift.
Let's have our friendship.

YOU AND ME

For now, I am without you, and you are without me.

The things we used to do are left alone to rot.
The bed is left unmade because
my hands can't reach the other side.

Our home is left unclean because
the songs we used to sing while sweeping
can't take my shattered voice.

And my tears are left unshed because
there's no one here to wipe them off and say,
"I'm here for you, my love. I'm everywhere for you."
I often find myself staring at our photographs.
They're everywhere, enormous wooden frames along
the walls, a couple seashell speckled ones

beneath the television, and even tiny ones
hidden in your bedside cabinet.
But my favorite one is still the same from twenty years ago.

In it, we are lying on the earth, surrounded
by the morning light and subtle sting of early winter air.
I remember you were telling me about

the way the clouds above us looked exactly
like a man and woman making love. In that moment,
there was nothing more important than listening to you.

It was after the flash of the camera that I saw love
for the first time, and I felt it when I held your hand and
       smiled.
That night, we went to your home and became the clouds.

I hope you're somewhere up there now, sitting
on a bench and telling others that
unfortunately, the seat next to you is taken.

I'm sorry, but I think I'll be a little late.
The bright yellow taxicab of Death may be outside,
but I am stuck reliving memories of you and me.

THE GIRL IN A BERET

I've almost forgotten you by now,
almost near the end
of that endless road.

Everything but that beret
atop your hazel head,
and the notebook that you held
in between your secrets and your ghosts.

I remember when my name
lined the pages of your heart,
a million times in violet and in gold.

I wonder if I'm nameless now,
turned into a storyline
or a simple crossed out word.

It's time for me to look ahead. The light
may burn, but I won't turn back any longer.

~~You~~

DEAR REM SLEEP

I know you help me sleep
and I know you mean your best,
but if I could make you stay away I would.
Don't be offended.
I just don't want to see her again,
not the way you show her to me.
Because you make me believe,
and I despise believing what you show me.
She never looked at me that way.
We never walked beneath the stars
in our bare feet, holding our hearts
in one hand and our shoes in the other.
We never kissed. We never felt
the happiness you think we did,
yet I believed it all when you came in
night after night to show me.
I cannot take any more of it.
I cannot take another vivid dream,
because no matter what I say,
I will always want to believe.
How could I not?
Even if I wake up and my vision
is blurry with tears
or if my voice abandons me as I scream,
I will always want to believe.
I hope you understand.
So please don't come tonight.
I'm far too weak, and I'm afraid
that the edge of my bed
is beginning to resemble the edge of a cliff,
and the waves below
are crashing against the hardwood floor.

IT'S YOU AGAIN TODAY

Hearts are broken everyday
-    Jewel Kilcher

I can imagine the look on your face
when you realize it's been shattered again.
Coming home from work to find it
lying in cement, half alive and splattered
everywhere. You'd reach for your chest and hopefor
anything, the whisper of a drum or the humming
of a note. Instead, there's only a cavity,
the same one you've reached for countless times.
Red faced and teary eyed, you'd bend over
and begin to pick it up. There's nothing in the world
that'll harm you more than cleaning up your heart
and realizing you were blind again. And as you
feel that weight once more you'll know that this time
there aren't any band aids left to fix it.
You'll know that this time you'll have to let it bleed
because truthfully, how else will you ever learn?

TONIGHT

I'll see you in my dreams tonight
Like time before
Your eyes so full of light

Asleep I'll feel your lips on mine
And wish for more
Our hands entwined like vines

You'll take my nights in full control
Forevermore
I'll yearn to touch your soul

You'll stay in dreams tonight and more
My heart is sore
For only dreams are doors

ORION

The grass is cold against my skin
and the stars above are mocking me,
pointing at my blinded eyes
and wounded skin.

They've seen the wretched truth,
witnessed it unfold under cover of the night.
You didn't love me, that much I could accept,
but why would you condemn me

to embarrassment and death?
Perhaps it is my own fault.
I should've been a little careful,
should've seen the hunters in the trees.

FORGET

I used to wish on shooting stars
for you, my dear, for you alone.
To kiss your lips and mend your scars,
to hear your laughs, your screams, your moans.
My only wish became a curse,
for you were barely wholly mine
when both our courage fled in turns,
and the sun, once bright, now didn't shine.
Yet still you stayed in thoughts and dreams
of day and night and all between.
I couldn't let you go, it seems,
although these thoughts to me were fiends.
It's time to leave this wish behind
and hide the stars that shine at night
in places none will ever find
so we can both escape this plight.
Forget her now, forget her soul.
Forget her grins, forget her frowns.
Forget this heavy Atlas toll.
Forget, forget, be free of bounds.

Acknowledgements

First, I'd like to thank Lauren Leung, who's immeasurable talent made the cover of this chapbook the beauty that it is. Thanks to Marcella Accardi as well, who helped me edit the early versions of these poems. To my parents, sister, and especially Sarah Schroll, who've believed in me for years. Thank you for all your kind words.

I'd like to thank you too, for reading this. It means the world to me.

ABOUT THE ARTIST

My name is Lauren Leung, and I designed the cover art for this exceptional book of poems. After weeks of preparing and brainstorming with the author, we came to an agreement for the cover art. I hope you enjoy my art and these poems.

ABOUT THE AUTHOR

Jose Cortes is currently a high school student in Illinois. He began writing poetry in freshman year, after a creative competition inspired him to do so. *Forget* is his first small project, but he doesn't plan to stop there. He both hopes and expects that you will see his name again sometime in the future not too far away.

Contact Info

If you would like to contact Jose, please reach out to him on Instagram: @iamonlywords.

If you would like to contact Lauren, please reach out to her on Instagram: @that_one_kid_aesthetic.